Digital File Organization

T.S. AVINI

Digital File Organization

A simple system to organize photos, documents, cloud storage, and computer clutter

by T. S. AVINI

Educational Disclaimer

This book is for educational and informational purposes only. It is not medical advice, diagnosis, treatment, or a substitute for care from a qualified healthcare professional. Always consult a licensed physician, dietitian, therapist, or other qualified professional before making changes to diet, exercise, supplements, medication, or treatment, especially if you have a medical condition, take medication, are pregnant, or have specific health concerns.

Financial Disclaimer

This book is for educational and informational purposes only. It is not financial, legal, tax, or investment advice. Personal finance decisions depend on individual circumstances. Consult a qualified financial, tax, or legal professional before making major financial decisions.

How to use this book: read one chapter at a time, choose one small practice, and apply it for a few days before moving forward. The goal is steady progress, not perfection.

Before you begin: use this book as a practical companion. You do not need to complete every exercise; focus on the sections that solve your most immediate problem.

Table of Contents

Chapter 1: Introduction to Digital File Organization: Understanding the Need for Order

In an increasingly digital world, the accumulation of files—photos from the latest family vacation, essential work documents, and the indispensable home budget spreadsheets—has become overwhelming. Whether stored on your laptop, smartphone, or in the cloud, the clutter can grow beyond manageable levels before you know it. The goal of this ebook is straightforward: to simplify the way you organize and manage these digital files, turning chaos into clarity.

The Modern Problem of Digital Clutter

Picture this: you need to find a specific document for a presentation that's about to start in ten minutes. In a perfect world, it would be just a few clicks away. But the reality often involves a frantic search through misnamed files and unstructured folders. This common scenario highlights the need for a coherent, reliable organizational system.

Digital clutter comes not only from our personal habits but also from technological advancements. As storage becomes cheaper and devices more capable, the temptation to save everything grows. However, without a strategy, this can lead to a mountain of unidentifiable files.

Common Symptoms of Digital Clutter:

- Lost Time: Spending several minutes or hours searching for files.
- Duplicate Files: Multiple copies of the same document or photo saved in different locations.
- Lack of Backup: Important files scattered across devices, making them hard to back up properly.
- Inefficiency: Wasting time organizing files on-the-fly instead of having them properly sorted initially.

Why Organization Matters

Just as a well-organized physical desk can help you focus on the task at hand, a structured digital environment enhances productivity and peace of mind. When your digital world is in order, you not only gain time but also alleviate stress. The mental drain of chaos is real, and a streamlined system can mitigate this.

Here's how an organized digital space makes your life easier:

- Improved Accessibility: A clear structure reduces the time spent searching for files, hence increasing efficiency.
- Enhanced Security: With files properly labeled and stored, setting up

backups and security systems becomes straightforward.

- Professional Appearance: Well-organized files reflect a well-organized mind, both in personal and professional arenas.
- Stress Reduction: Decluttered digital spaces contribute to a clearer mental space, freeing you from the anxiety of a chaotic file system.

Reflecting on Your Current System

Before diving into new methods, it's essential to understand your baseline. Evaluating your current practices gives you insights into what works, what doesn't, and what could be improved. Take a moment to reflect:

- Do you have a filing system, or is everything stored where it lands?
- How often do you spend time looking for files?
- Have you ever lost an important document or photo due to poor organization?

Let's turn introspection into action with some exercises.

Mini Exercise: Evaluate Your Current Situation

- Select a Device: Choose one device that you frequently use (e.g., laptop, smartphone).
- Inventory Assessment: List the types of files you commonly store (e.g., photos, work documents, personal projects).
- Identify Pain Points: Note where you usually face issues (e.g., finding documents, running out of storage space).
- Goal Setting: Define what an ideal digital space looks like for you. Is it fewer folders, better naming conventions, or more use of cloud services?

Spending even a brief moment on these points can set you on the path to better digital management.

Crafting a Personal Filing System

As you start building or refining a system, let's go through some essentials to keep in mind:

- Folder Structure: Think of your digital files like a filing cabinet. Each drawer represents a broad category (e.g., Work, Personal, Finances). Inside each drawer, folders should represent specific areas or projects (e.g., Reports, Correspondence, Taxes).
- Naming Conventions: Standardized naming conventions can make files easy to find. Use clear and relevant file names, including dates and categories if possible (e.g., 2023_Financial_Report_Q1.pdf).
- Regular Review: Just as you would with a fridge or wardrobe, periodically reviewing your files ensures your system remains functional. Dedicate time

monthly or quarterly to declutter and reorganize.

• Cloud Usage: With the free and paid options available, cloud storage solves several logistical problems. It offers both a backup solution and the convenience of accessing your files from any device.

Practical Checklist for Organizing Files:

• Set up broad category folders for each area of your life.

• Develop a naming convention that includes the key details (project name, date, version).

• Commit to a regular schedule to review and clean up files – monthly is a great start.

• Evaluate cloud storage options and integrate them into your system.

Building Habits for the Long Term

A system is only as good as the habits supporting it. Building new habits involves consistency and patience. Here are some advice pointers to keep your digital space orderly:

• Create an "Actions" folder where you can briefly drop files to sort later. But ensure you schedule time to clear it out regularly.

• Develop a quick daily routine for file sorting. The more automatic this process becomes, the less mental effort it requires.

• Celebrate small wins. Acknowledge the clarity and time savings you gain by having an organized digital world.

The journey to mastering digital file organization might start with sorting through layers of existing clutter, but the rewards—efficiency, reduced stress, and enhanced productivity—are well worth it. Each file you organize is a step toward a more manageable and productive digital life. By embracing the need for order, you're not only clearing up your digital landscape but also creating space for more creativity and focus in your life.

Chapter 2: The Digital Mess: Identifying Your Personal Pain Points

Today's digital landscape, bustling with diversity and data, is a double-edged sword. While technology enhances productivity and creativity, it can also lead to an overwhelming clutter of files, photos, and documents—akin to a digital junkyard. The key to reclaiming your digital space begins with understanding the personal pain points that lead to this chaos. In this chapter, we'll embark on a journey to identify these digital mess organizers, tailored to your unique experiences and habits.

Recognizing Your Digital Disarray

The first step to addressing any mess is acknowledging it exists. Digital clutter often sneaks up on us, concealed by flashy app interfaces and powerful processors. You may notice this mess when searching for a document takes longer than creating it anew, or when photo folders resemble a chaotic gallery rather than a curated album. The moment organizing your digital world feels burdensome, take it as a sign to delve deeper.

Understanding Root Causes

For many, the digital mess grows from a forest of unaddressed habits Identifying your specific triggers can help you tackle the problem at its core. Here are some common root causes of digital disarray:

- File Hoarding : Keeping every version of every file, just in case, contributes to an unmanageable mass of data. Reflect on whether you truly need fifteen drafts of the same document.
- Procrastination : Putting off organizing until later can transform a few misplaced files into a system-wide sprawl. Aim to file ethically—a minute now saves hours later.
- Over-reliance on Search Functions : Trusting search tools instead of knowing where files are stored may breed laziness in file management. While search functions are supportive, a structured folder system adds clarity and speed.

Suspending judgment while analyzing these habits is crucial. Acknowledge the triggers as they are, understanding that it's common to develop these patterns without realizing their impact on productivity.

Exercises for Self-Inventory

Much like any organizational endeavor, understanding what you have is key. Here are some exercises to recognize your clutter:

- Digital Detox : As a starting exercise, spend 15 minutes scrolling through your files. Note where you naturally go first versus the scattered regions you ignore. Pay attention to what surprises you—unexpected duplicates, ancient downloads, or archival photos. This initial sweep offers insights without diving deep just yet.

• File Counting : Pick a folder or file type (such as PDFs or images), and count how many you have. Use this insight to judge whether the number feels justified.

• Day in the Life : Map out a typical day and note moments when digital clutter interferes. Is it a struggle finding meeting notes? Do you grapple with packed inboxes? Recognizing disruption points helps target improvements.

Personalizing Your Approach

No universal digital organization method applies to everyone, as each person's digital expression varies widely. To tailor a system for you, it helps to ask reflective questions:

• Which types of files matter most to my personal or professional goals?

• Are there applications or devices that complicate rather than facilitate my digital life?

• What feelings frequently arise when I engage with my digital environment—stress, contentment, confusion?

With these reflections, strive to build a system that resonates with your habits. Maybe it's about setting up dedicated weekly times for sorting, or perhaps it's leveraging applications geared towards your specific professional needs.

Getting Creative with Solutions

While standard folder structures and naming conventions are useful, thinking outside the box can offer tailored solutions:

• Virtual Date Night : Establish a monthly session focusing solely on digital cleanup. Set the ambiance with music to break from routine and see it as a valuable ritual rather than a chore.

• Cross-device Synchronization : Configure settings that effortlessly sync your devices. When your phone and laptop communicate seamlessly, it ensures your digital workplace remains streamlined.

• Visual Organizing Tools : Consider applications like Trello or Milanote for visually inclined users. Such tools transform a plain list into a vibrant map, making navigation intuitive.

Reflection and Adjustment

As with any habit change, patience and persistence are paramount. Engage in regular reflection to see what works and what doesn't. The great news is that your digital environment is adaptable. As you grow professionally and personally, so can your organizational strategies.

Think of this chapter as the preamble to a more structured digital existence. By identifying and addressing your unique digital pain points, you set the stage for every subsequent chapter of this book to resonate more meaningfully. As we journey together, continue embracing trial and the occasional error. After all, in recognizing the mess, you've taken a significant step towards clarity and control.

Chapter 3: Mastering the Basics: File Naming Conventions and Hierarchies

There's a unique satisfaction in knowing exactly where your digital files reside, how they are named, and how effortlessly you can retrieve them when needed. In today's fast-paced digital world, having a robust system for organizing files is not just a luxury; it's a necessity. This chapter aims to guide you through the foundational steps of creating a personalized and efficient structure using file naming conventions and hierarchies, with the promise of bringing clarity to your digital space.

The Art of Naming Your Files Right

Let's begin with file naming conventions, an underappreciated yet critical element in any file organization strategy. A good file naming system can save you from the exasperation of opening multitudes of files to find what you need. It helps you maintain an intuitive system that remains consistent over time.

Why Does File Naming Matter?

Imagine trying to find a lone sock in a sea of identical clothing items. It's frustrating and time-consuming. A similar chaos unfolds with poorly named files. Conversely, meaningful names can facilitate rapid file retrieval and help keep your ecosystem orderly. Here's what effective file names can do for you:

• Increase Search Efficiency: Meaningful file names allow your computer's search capabilities to accurately find the needed file.

• Ensure Consistency: Provides a harmonious system where everything has its place, reducing the need to constantly reorganize.

• Enhance Collaboration: Shared file systems are more intuitive when everyone follows the same naming conventions.

Best Practices for File Naming

• Be Descriptive but Concise: Aim for file names that summarize the content without becoming too lengthy. For example, using "2023_Q1_ExpenseReport.pdf" is more effective than "Report1.pdf."

• Include Dates: When applicable, incorporating a date in a uniform format (YYYY-MM-DD) can help chronologically order files, making them easier to locate later.

• Standardize Terminology: Avoid misconceptions by using a consistent vocabulary. If you use 'Invoice' for billing documents, don't switch to 'Bill' or 'Billing.'

• Logical Sequence: Decide on the order of elements in your file name. Choose the most important characteristic to appear first, like "ClientName_ProjectName_Version."

- Utilize underscores or dashes: Spaces in file names can cause issues across different systems. Use underscores (_) or dashes (-) to separate words.
- Version Control: When dealing with iterative documents, include a version number or timestamp, such as “v2” or “2023-05-update.”

Exercise: Take a moment to review a list of recent documents. Do they follow a consistent naming pattern? If not, how might you rename them for better clarity?

Structuring Through Hierarchies

File hierarchies, much like a well-organized closet, provide spatial order to an otherwise flat landscape. By leveraging a logical folder structure, you'll set up a navigation system to efficiently accompany your file naming convention.

The Importance of Hierarchies

Much like the Dewey Decimal System in a library, a solid file hierarchy can efficiently house a multitude of documents while offering an easy retrieval system. Benefits include:

- Reduced Clutter: A clear structure minimizes the accumulation of unnecessary files.
- Better Focus: When every document has its place, you can focus more easily on the task at hand.
- Efficient Collaboration: In shared environments, a unified structure ensures files are easy to locate and update.

Building Your File Hierarchy

- Identify Categories: Start with broad categories that apply to your life or work — for a business, this could be Administration, Projects, Finance.
- Subdivide Rationally: Under each top-level category, create subfolders that capture detailed elements. In Projects, you might subdivide by client or project name.
- Consistent Naming: Align folder names with your file naming conventions for coherence.
- Archive Completed Projects: Once a project is finished, archive it in a dedicated Archive folder to maintain a clutter-free workspace.
- Review and Revise: Periodically assess the hierarchy's effectiveness. Does it still make sense? Is it intuitive? Update as needed.

Practical Example: Suppose you're a graphic designer. Your high-level folders could include ClientWork, Templates, and Personal_Projects. Under ClientWork, create individual folders for each client, and within those, folders named for specific projects or years.

Common Pitfalls and How to Avoid Them

While creating an efficient file organization system isn't overly complex, it's not immune to common mistakes. Here are some pitfalls to avoid:

• Overcomplicating the System: If a system is too complex, it becomes cumbersome. Aim for simplicity.

• Ignoring Consistency: Inconsistent naming conventions and folder systems cause confusion and inefficiency.

• Neglecting Maintenance: A set-it-and-forget-it approach can lead to digital clutter. Regularly clean out unnecessary files and reevaluate the hierarchy.

• Omitting Backup Plans: An organized file system is useless if data is lost. Ensure your files are backed up regularly, either in cloud storage or via external drives.

Checklist for Effective File Systems

• [ ] Develop a set of clear, descriptive file naming conventions.

• [ ] Establish a logical hierarchy that caters to your unique needs.

• [ ] Consistently review and update both naming and structural conventions.

• [ ] Implement a backup system and stick to it.

• [ ] Foster a routine practice of decluttering and archiving as necessary.

By following these guidelines, you create a standardized, user-friendly framework tailored to your personal or professional life, making file management less of a chore and more of a seamless part of your daily routine. Embark on this organizational journey with these practical tips, and you'll liberate yourself from digital chaos, creating an environment where your files are just as reliable and accessible as your most trusted organizational tools.

Chapter 4: Essential Tools for File Management: Software and Apps to Consider

Navigating the digital landscape of file management doesn't need to feel like steering a ship through a storm without a compass. With the right tools, even the most cluttered digital spaces can be transformed into models of efficiency. In this chapter, we'll explore a variety of software and apps designed to make organizing your photos, documents, and other digital files a breeze. Our goal is to help you determine which tools align with your specific needs, ensuring a smoother, more intuitive file management journey.

Finding the Right Tools for You

Before diving in, it's essential to reflect on your particular file management needs. Are you an avid photographer with thousands of images to sort? A professional maintaining a complex library of documents? Understanding your primary requirements will help guide your choice of tools, preventing you from feeling overwhelmed by the wide array of options.

File Management Software: A Closer Look

Different tools serve different purposes, and here, we will break them down:

• General File Organization:

• Explorer (Windows) / Finder (MacOS):

These built-in tools are your digital file cabinets. They offer basic organization features, such as file naming, folder creation, and searching capabilities. Learning shortcut keys can enhance efficiency. For instance, 'Ctrl + C' to copy and 'Ctrl + V' to paste in Windows, or 'Command + C' and 'Command + V' on a Mac, make handling files faster.

• Total Commander:

For those who want a more robust Windows experience, Total Commander offers dual-pane views and advanced search functionality. It's a throwback to the days of Norton Commander, only with modern conveniences.

• Photo Management:

• Adobe Lightroom:

Widely regarded as the gold standard for photographers, Lightroom combines powerful editing tools with robust file organization capabilities. You can tag, rate, and categorize photos within intuitive catalogs. For those managing large volumes of photos, the ability to batch rename and apply metadata is invaluable.

• Google Photos:

Perfect for casual users, Google Photos offers cloud storage and organization without additional software. Its AI-powered capabilities automatically categorize photos, and it integrates seamlessly with other Google services.

- Document Management:
- Evernote:

Ideal for personal and professional document management, Evernote allows you to capture ideas, scan documents, and categorize information using notebooks and tags. Its search function even recognizes handwritten text in scanned notes, adding a layer of convenience for on-the-go management.

- Microsoft OneDrive:

This option is particularly beneficial for Windows users looking for cloud-based synchronization. OneDrive syncs documents across devices, offering seamless access to files whether on a computer, tablet, or smartphone.

Cloud Storage Solutions: Keeping Files Accessible

Cloud storage is an integral part of modern file management, providing accessibility and backup options that protect against data loss.

- Dropbox:

Known for its simplicity and reliability, Dropbox facilitates easy synchronization across multiple devices. It's a versatile tool that professionals rely on for both file sharing and backup.

- iCloud Drive:

For Apple ecosystem devotees, iCloud Drive delivers an effortless integration with Macs, iPhones, and iPads. It backs up photos and documents automatically, ensuring they are available across all devices.

Exercise: Choosing Your Cloud Solution

Reflect on your current device usage. Are you entrenched in the Apple universe, or do you use a mix of operating systems? Consider what you need most from cloud storage—be it large volume storage, document collaboration, or just a reliable backup option—and select a service that aligns with these needs.

Avoiding Common Pitfalls

Even with the best tools, missteps can occur. Here's how to avoid them:

- Overcomplicating Structures:

While nesting folders can seem like a good idea, it often leads to buried files that are difficult to find. Opt instead for a simple yet meaningful naming convention.

- Neglecting to Back Up:

Even with cloud solutions, regularly backing up your files to an external hard drive is a wise practice. It's a small step that can save immense time and stress in the event of a cloud service outage or data corruption.

• Ignoring Automation Features:

Modern software often includes automation features. In Lightroom, for example, you can set up import presets that apply to every batch of photos, streamlining your workflow.

Building Your Personal System

A systematic approach to file management combines thoughtful tool selection with strategic habits. Consider the following checklist as you develop your personal system:

• Audit Your Current Situation:

Evaluate your existing file organization. Identify what works and what areas need improvement.

• Define Your Goals:

Are you looking to streamline accessibility, enhance sharing capabilities, or simply declutter? Understanding your goals will shape your system.

• Commit to Regular Maintenance:

Set aside time monthly to review and reorganize your files. Regular maintenance prevents clutter from accumulating and ensures that your system remains effective.

Reflection Prompt

Consider a time when you struggled to find a digital file. What caused the difficulty, and how can the tools and strategies discussed in this chapter prevent similar issues in the future? Reflecting on your past experiences can be an enlightening step toward a more organized digital life.

By considering these tools and tips, you can create an environment where files are not just stored, but strategically managed, ensuring peace of mind and enhanced productivity as you navigate your digital world.

Chapter 5: Organizing Digital Photos: Techniques for Efficient Sorting and Storing

In an age where phones double as cameras and the world is accessible through a lens, digital photo accumulation happens almost effortlessly. A thousand pictures of your adorable pet might seem just right until you can't find that charming snap you want to show your friends. Organizing digital photos is not only about keeping aesthetic order but also about creating a system where moments are easily retrievable, and devices don't creak under the weight of burgeoning galleries. This chapter is your introduction to reclaiming control over your digital photo treasures.

Why Organize?

Before diving into techniques, consider why organizing photos matters. Imagine preparing an album for a loved one's milestone birthday—without a system, the task would be overwhelming. Good organization means you can quickly locate photos, enjoy your memories without stress, and even improve device performance by reducing excess storage usage. When your digital photos are sorted, they become accessible memories, not burdens.

The Digital Decluttering Mindset

Approach the task with patience. Sorting through digital photos is akin to sorting through an attic—it's layered, emotive, and at times nostalgic. But with each selection and deletion, you strengthen your organizational resolve. Set aside time specifically for this task—perhaps an hour each weekend—to avoid fatigue and make consistent progress. This mindset shift from chore to opportunity to reminisce can make the process enjoyable rather than tiresome.

Process Blueprint for Sorting Photos

• Collect and Consolidate : Begin by bringing all your digital photos into one place. This might mean downloading pictures from various accounts (Google Photos, iCloud, etc.) and devices (phones, tablets, cameras). Aim to have every snapshot accessible on a single device or external drive.

• Set Up a Primary Storage Location : Choose a central storage spot. For many, this means a high-capacity external hard drive or a dedicated cloud storage account. This location is your digital archive.

• Create a Simple Folder System : Efficient folder structures are the backbone of photo organization. Here are some suggested ways to structure folders:

• Date-Based : Year > Month > Event (e.g., 2023 > July > Family Reunion)

• Event-Based : Vacations > 2023 Ski Trip

• Category-Based : Friends, Family, Travel

Tip : Designate an "Unsorted" folder as a temporary hold for new or unsorted photos to tackle later.

Techniques for Sorting

- Tagging and Keywords : Software like Adobe Lightroom allows for photo tagging, which is immensely useful for cross-referencing images that belong to multiple categories (e.g., "Beach Vacation" and "Family").
- Rating and Culling : Many apps allow you to "star" or rate photos, helping you quickly identify the best shots. Develop a criterion—for instance, 1 star for keep, 5 stars for showcase—and keep only your favorites.
- Delete Ruthlessly : Duplicates and blurs are clutter culprits. Free up space by regularly pruning these out. As a rule of thumb: If a photo doesn't evoke an emotion or capture an important moment, it might be safe to let it go.

A Short Exercise: Memory Lane Miracle

- Take an hour and select any folder or set of photos.
- Aim to cull the collection by at least 15%.
- As you remove duplicates or poor shots, set aside a few treasured ones in a new folder named "Top 10 Memories." This folder showcases highlights and reminds you of the joy behind the organization.

Tools and Tips for Easy Maintenance

- Automated Uploads : Services like Google Photos or Apple Photos offer automatic photo back-up. While useful, ensure you're not doubling up and creating new disorganized messes.
- Regular Backups : Consistency is key. Dedicate time, perhaps monthly, to back up new photos to your primary storage location. This avoids mishaps and data loss.

Common Pitfalls to Avoid

- Overcomplicating Systems : Simplicity is your friend. An overly complex system discourages maintenance.
- Neglecting Security : Always ensure your storage solutions are secure, particularly cloud-based ones, by using strong passwords and two-factor authentication where possible.
- Procrastination : Delaying organization leads to overwhelm. Break tasks into manageable sessions to maintain momentum.

Reflective Prompt: Personal Photo Philosophy

Take a moment to reflect: What do your digital photos mean to you? Is it capturing moments with loved ones, documenting travel adventures, or preserving artistic endeavors? Understanding this can guide your organization strategy and ensure it remains personally meaningful.

Organizing digital photos isn’t just about managing data—it's about creating a path through the stories of your life. With these techniques, what seemed a daunting digital heap can transform into an accessible, joy-inducing collection. Your pictures deserve to be seen; let them have the spotlight they rightfully earned.

Chapter 6: Managing Digital Documents: Best Practices for Papers and PDFs

In the digital age, our computers and cloud storage spaces have become the new filing cabinets. Where once we juggled physical papers, now we face an overflow of digital documents and PDFs, threatening to clutter our desktops and overwhelm our mental bandwidth. Organizing these documents doesn't have to be a Herculean task. With some thoughtful strategies, you can create a streamlined, efficient system that enhances both personal productivity and peace of mind.

The Foundation of Digital Document Management

The first step is understanding what digital documents constitute. They include everything from receipts and bills to reports, essays, and e-books. Knowing what you have is half the battle. Start by performing a digital audit—spend time identifying what types of documents you save and where they reside, such as folders on your desktop, your downloads folder, or various cloud services.

Once you've mapped out your digital landscape, it's essential to consolidate these files into a central hub. Whether it's a dedicated folder on your computer or a cloud storage solution like Google Drive or Dropbox, centralizing your documents allows for more accessible organization and retrieval.

Naming Conventions That Make Sense

A critical aspect of organizing your digital documents is adopting clear and consistent naming conventions. A well-crafted naming system will reduce the time you spend searching and eliminate the likelihood of losing important files in an ocean of similarly named documents.

- Be Descriptive : Incorporate keywords that tell you exactly what the file contains (e.g., "2023_Tax_Return").
- Use Dates : Include dates in the file name to sort and find documents related to specific time frames (e.g., "Meeting_Notes_2023-04-15").
- Standardize Format : Pick a format and stick with it. Consistency is crucial—deciding on "yyyy-mm-dd" for dates, for instance, can become a personal standard.

This attention to detail is invaluable when searching or using sorting functions.

Folder Hierarchy: Building Your Digital Filing Cabinet

With names under control, the next step is establishing an intuitive folder hierarchy. Simplicity is key. Your folders should act as broad categories under which your documents naturally fit, much like you would organize physical papers.

Consider creating top-level folders that reflect major areas of your life or work. Here are some examples to help spark your thinking:

- Personal : Bills, health records, personal letters.
- Work : Reports, meeting notes, presentations.
- Finance : Bank statements, investment documents, tax information.
- Education : Educational certificates, assignments, research papers.

Within each of these categories, subfolders can house more specific document types ("2023 Invoices," "Quarterly Reports," etc.). Just remember the golden rule—paths should ideally run three or four folders deep to prevent unnecessary complexity.

The PDF Problem: Tips for Handling Portable Document Format Files

PDFs, while useful for maintaining the format consistency of documents across devices, present their own challenges. They are the primary format for scanned documents and often carry essential information. Here are some practical tips for managing them effectively:

- OCR Tools : Use Optical Character Recognition (OCR) tools to make scanned documents searchable. This is especially helpful when dealing with text-heavy documents like contracts or printed materials that have been scanned.
- Merge and Split : Take advantage of PDF merging tools to combine related documents into a single file, and splitting tools to cut larger PDFs into more manageable sections for collaboration or reference.
- Compression : Large PDF files can quickly consume storage space. Employ compression tools which reduce file size without sacrificing quality.

Avoiding Common Pitfalls in Digital Document Management

Now that your files are organized and methods established, maintaining this system is the next challenge. Here, vigilance is essential:

- Regular Reviews : Schedule periodic checks to ensure folders are tidy and files are in their proper places. Delete what's no longer necessary. Monthly reviews often suffice for moderate document volume.
- Backups Are Essential : Regularly back up your documents. This could be to an external hard drive or a secondary cloud service. Use automation tools to schedule backups, ensuring that they occur consistently.

Establishing a Routine

Finally, ease for future maintenance with a routine. Made part of a daily or weekly practice, maintenance becomes second nature:

- At the end of each workday or week, spend a few minutes sorting any new digital documents.

• Make it a habit to name and file digital documents as soon as they are created or received.

Reflection Prompts for Improvement

Incorporating a routine is the beginning of creating a digital document management system that works seamlessly for you. Reflect on these prompts to continue optimizing your approach:

• What types of documents do you most often save, and are they easily accessible?

• Are there documents that frequently go missing? How can your system be adapted to prevent such occurrences?

• How could your naming conventions or folder hierarchy be more intuitive?

• How often are you deviating from your organization system, and why?

By leveraging these strategies and maintaining an adaptive routine, you can transform the task of managing digital documents from a chaotic challenge into a streamlined process that frees up mental space and enhances productivity. As the digital landscape continues to evolve, having a personal system in place is not just practical; it's essential.

Chapter 7: Conquering Cloud Storage: Maximizing Space and Security

The digital world is both a blessing and a challenge. With endless possibilities to store photos, documents, and memories, cloud storage has become an essential tool. However, without proper management, it can quickly become a digital junkyard. This chapter will guide you through maximizing space and ensuring the security of your files in the cloud—a place that's as cloudy for many as it is convenient.

Understanding the Basics

Let's start by understanding what cloud storage is and how it works. Essentially, it's a service that allows you to save data on external servers managed by a third-party provider. This can liberate your local device's memory, offering flexibility and accessibility from anywhere with an internet connection. Popular services like Google Drive, iCloud, Dropbox, and OneDrive each offer unique features and varying storage limits. Knowing your options will empower you to choose the best fit for your needs.

Embrace Minimalism

Start with a Cleaning Session : Before uploading files to the cloud, take a moment to sift through your digital stuff. Just as you wouldn't store moldy clothes in your closet, don't upload unnecessary files. Assess what you truly need—this might mean keeping high-quality photos of family events and letting go of blurry duplicates or screenshots of memes.

Categorize and Consolidate : Organizing your files into clear categories and folders is vital. Think of your cloud as a closet. Would you throw everything in haphazardly? Effective categorization avoids clutter and facilitates a more streamlined retrieval process. Create distinct folders for work documents, personal photos, creative projects, and important copies of identification or certifications.

Maximize Your Space

Leverage Built-In Features : Make the most out of the features provided by your cloud service. Google Photos, for instance, automatically backs up your phone's photos, offering a 'High Quality' option that compresses images to maintain good quality without eating into your storage quota. Dropbox's 'Smart Sync' feature helps store files online-only, saving precious local disk space.

Shared Storage Plans : If your family or business already uses a cloud service, look into family plans or business agreements. These plans often offer more gigabytes for the buck and make it easy to manage storage under one account, reducing duplicated efforts and data.

Prioritize Security

Protective Measures : Security is paramount when placing sensitive information online. Always enable two-factor authentication to add an extra layer of security. This means that even if someone obtains your password, they would still need a secondary verification code sent to your device.

Regularly Update Passwords : Hackers often exploit outdated passwords. Set reminders to update your passwords at least every six months. Use complex passwords that mix numbers, symbols, and upper- and lowercase letters, or consider using a reliable password manager to keep things both secure and accessible.

Beware of Phishing Scams : Being cautious initially can save a lot of headaches. Be skeptical of any unsolicited messages asking for your login information, no matter how official they appear. Check the email addresses and verify any suspicious activity directly on your cloud provider's site rather than clicking links in an email.

Creating a Backup System

Have a Local Backup : While cloud storage is convenient, technology can fail. Ensure that you have a local backup of critical files on an external hard drive. This is particularly crucial for invaluable items such as family photos or important business documents.

Consider Redundancy : For peace of mind, use more than one cloud storage provider. Keeping essential files in at least two independent locations—say Google Drive and OneDrive—increases accessibility and provides a safety net in case of service outages.

Reflection Exercise

Spend a few moments pondering over your digital possessions. How often have you uploaded files impulsively, only to forget them days later? Reflect on your current cloud arrangement. Ask yourself:

• Are my current folders and files logically organized?

• Which files have I not accessed in the past year—do I truly need them?

• Do I feel confident about the security of my files, or do I need to take additional steps?

These reflections will provide clarity and direction, ensuring that your cloud storage remains a useful resource, not a digital swamp.

Practical Tips

• Routine Checks : Schedule a monthly check-in with your cloud storage. Delete redundant or obsolete files regularly to maintain efficiency.

• Document Naming Conventions : Adopt a consistent and clear naming convention for your files. For example, date-sensitive documents might start with the year-month-day format (YYYYMMDD) for easy sorting.

• Labels and Tags : Utilize tags or labels if your cloud service allows them. This way, even if a file straddles two categories, searching becomes a breeze.

Chapter Takeaway

Mastering cloud storage doesn't require a revolutionary mindset. Instead, it calls for regular maintenance, secure practices, and a thoughtful approach to what you keep and where you store it. By following these guidelines, you'll transform your cloud storage from a chaotic assortment into an organized, secure repository that's easy to navigate. Remember, less is often more—not just in your living room but in the digital cloud as well.

Chapter 8: Decluttering Your Downloads: Strategies for Managing a Common Chaos Zone

The downloads folder on your computer can often become the digital equivalent of a junk drawer. You know the one—it's the catch-all for everything you didn't have time to put away properly. Overstuffed with random PDFs from last week's webinar, vacation pictures, and the odd software update file, this folder often becomes a chaotic nightmare where finding anything is a task in itself. Let's explore how to tame this chaotic zone by applying a few practical strategies that, once implemented, will save you time, stress, and the inevitable frustration of not finding your files when you need them.

Understanding the Root of the Chaos

Before diving into solutions, it's important to understand why the downloads folder can become such a mess. Most browsers and applications save downloaded files here by default, providing a convenient temporary home. However, when temporary solutions become permanent habits, clutter ensues. Recognize the downloads folder for what it ideally should be: a stopping point rather than a storage location. This slight mindset shift is crucial, as it sets the stage for maintaining order.

The Quick Sort: Implementing Immediate Actions

When tackling a cluttered downloads folder, a quick initial sort can make a dramatic difference. Allocate a focused 15-30 minutes and go through the following steps:

- Delete the Duplicates : Use the built-in search function to find and remove duplicate files. This is often one of the quickest routes to reducing clutter.
- Remove Installation Files : After software is successfully installed and running, its setup files are usually unnecessary. Make sure everything is working and then feel free to delete these.
- Archive Completed Projects : For files related to completed tasks or projects, create a folder elsewhere on your computer or external storage to save them. This can be a "2019 Completed Projects" folder within your Documents or on an external drive.

A System for Ongoing Maintenance

Creating a functional and sustainable system involves defining a simple set of rules and practices you can easily follow long-term. Here are core strategies to maintain your downloads folder:

- Designate Specific File Destinations : Modify browser and application settings to ask where to save each file or automatically place downloads in designated folders (e.g., photos to the Images folder or PDFs to Documents). This reduces the number of files piling up in Downloads in the first place.

• Weekly or Monthly Routine : Set aside regular time, whether weekly or monthly as per your file download frequency, for a quick maintenance check. This involves clearing redundant downloads and ensuring any useful files are moved to their respective folders.

• Temporary Storage System : Create subfolders within Downloads for items you genuinely need short-term. For instance, create "Temporary" for items deleted within a week or "Review Later" for material you'd like to go over. Make it routine to clear them out.

Dealing with Common Mistakes

One common error people make is keeping the mindset that bigger is better when it comes to storage space, often leading to a 'stash all and forget' mentality. To counteract this, operate under the principle that just because it doesn't take physical space, doesn't mean it won't take mental space. Each file should justify its existence on your computer, either by current relevance or long-term necessity.

Another pitfall is procrastination—it's easy to tell yourself you'll sort your downloads later. Counteract this by leveraging reminders or calendar alerts to establish a decluttering routine. When you make the process regular and manageable, it doesn't become overwhelming.

Technology to the Rescue

Technology can significantly simplify maintaining a clean downloads folder. Here are some digital tools and features to assist:

• Automatic File Management Apps : Tools such as Hazel (Mac) or DropIt (Windows) can automatically sort files into folders based on the rules you set. They're powerful allies in maintaining order.

• Browser Extensions : Utilize extensions that optimize downloads management. Extensions can prompt you to sort downloads immediately or better organize file-saving habits directly from your browser.

• Built-in Sort Functions : Many operating systems offer built-in features to sort files by type, date, or size. Use these to quickly visualize what's taking up space and what can be effortlessly sorted or removed.

Exercise: Reflect and Act

Set 20 minutes on your calendar for a downloads folder decluttering session. Use the guideline provided above or these prompts to begin:

• Look through your downloads and apply the "one-year rule": If you haven't used or needed it in over a year, consider removing it.

• Examine your recent downloads and categorize them. What do you notice?

What types of files keep appearing, and where should they ideally be moved?

• Implement one small change in your download habits starting today (e.g., changing the default save location for certain files).

Wrapping Up

Successfully managing your downloads folder comes down to habit overhauls, system adjustments, and consistent maintenance. This clutter-free approach isn't just about aesthetics or finding files quickly. It's about reclaiming control over your digital space and reducing that underlying current of stress caused by digital disorder. With these strategies and a little patience, you can transform your downloads folder from a chaos zone to a streamlined, efficient space.

Chapter 9: Email Attachment Management: Streamlining Your Inbox and Beyond

Imagine opening your email inbox and feeling a wave of calm rather than panic at the barrage of attachments mixed with messages. The difference? A well-organized approach to managing email attachments that complements the overall strategy of digital file organization. In this chapter, we'll delve into how you can turn that vision into reality with pragmatic steps and thoughtful reflection on how to streamline your inbox and beyond.

The Case for Organized Attachments

Email attachments, both sent and received, tend to accumulate over time, creating digital clutter that can become overwhelming. Not to mention the unnecessary space they consume in your email storage. But there's more at stake: effectively managed attachments prevent the chances of losing crucial information, ensure easier accessibility, and improve productivity.

Taking Stock: Reflective Audit

Start with a simple exercise: conduct a 'reflective audit' of your current attachment habits. Ask yourself:

- How often do I download attachments directly from emails?
- How many times have I struggled to find a file because it was buried in an old email?
- Do I have a system to regularly clean and store important attachments?

Jot down your observations. Understanding your habits is the first step toward improving them.

Streamlining with Systems

To begin with managing your email attachments effectively, consider the following strategies:

- Designate a Download Folder : Create a dedicated folder on your computer or cloud storage titled "Email Attachments" for easy access.
- Use Tags and Folders Within Your Email : Utilize your email's tagging or folder system to categorize attachments by project, client, or date. For instance, create subfolders named "2023 Tax Documents" or "Project Alpha."
- Set Up Automatic Filters : Most email services allow you to set up filters that automate the categorization of incoming emails, helping you to immediately categorize and archive emails with attachments.

Quick Wins: Immediate Actions

- Daily Downloads : Make it a habit to download attachments you need and organize them into the designated folder right away. This prevents your inbox from becoming a filing cabinet.

• Consistent Naming Conventions : When saving attachments, use consistent naming conventions. Label files by their content, date, and importance to ensure clarity.

• Weekly Cleanup : Dedicate 15 minutes each week to go through your most recent emails and confirm that new attachments have been saved and organized accordingly. Use this opportunity to delete those that you don't need anymore.

Mini Exercise: Categorization Practice

Take the next 10 emails with attachments in your inbox. Download the attachments and save them in your designated download folder.

• Sort by Priority : Identify which files are crucial, which are of moderate importance, and which are not essential.

• Categorize : Move each file to the appropriate subfolder within your "Email Attachments" folder.

• Delete Permanently : If any files are redundant or outdated, delete them permanently from your email as well as your storage.

Reflect on how this exercise made you feel about managing your email attachments. Did it simplify your inbox?

Cloud Storage: Your Best Ally

Sometimes, the volume of your email attachments requires more than local storage solutions. Here's where cloud storage services come in handy:

• Direct Saving from Inbox : Use integrations offered by your email service with cloud storage providers like Google Drive or Dropbox to save attachments directly from your inbox.

• Automatic Backups : Consider setting up systems where all attachments in specific categories are automatically backed up in cloud storage.

Avoiding Common Mistakes

When organizing email attachments, the pitfalls are familiar:

• Neglecting Regular Organization Tasks : It's easy to save files and then forget about them. Set reminders to organize your email downloads regularly.

• Ignoring Privacy and Security Concerns : Be cautious when saving sensitive documents. Ensure your files are stored in secure, password-protected folders, especially when using cloud storage.

• Over-cluttering with Irrelevance : Mindfully evaluate the importance of each attachment. Don't be afraid to delete non-essential files.

Practical Checklist: Email Attachment Management

- [ ] Create and label a dedicated folder for email attachments.
- [ ] Establish a consistent naming system for saved files.
- [ ] Utilize email folders and tags for easy navigation.
- [ ] Set up email filters for incoming attachments.
- [ ] Conduct a weekly review and cleanup of your email attachments.
- [ ] Leverage cloud storage for large volumes or sensitive documents.
- [ ] Implement security measures for sensitive attachments.

Optimizing how you manage email attachments might seem like a small step in the grand scheme of digital organization, but its impact is substantial. It not only helps in maintaining a tidier inbox but also ensures that important documents are always within easy reach. With these practices in place, your digital landscape becomes more navigable, allowing you to focus on what truly matters: productivity without the clutter. By translating this focused attention to other areas of your digital life, you'll find pathways to clarity and efficiency you might not have thought possible before.

Chapter 10: Creating a Centralized Filing System: Bringing Order to Disparate Files

In today's digital age, where our lives are scattered across phones, laptops, tablets, and cloud services, managing files might seem like maneuvering through a chaotic forest with no clear path. You may feel overwhelmed just thinking about all the photos, documents, and digital snippets saved in several locations. This chapter aims to guide you in creating a centralized filing system, a straightforward solution that brings harmony and efficiency. No more endless searches or lost files; it's time to enjoy the serenity of a well-organized digital life.

Why Centralization Matters

Before diving into the process, it's important to grasp why a centralized filing system is beneficial. Primarily, it prevents the headache of searching through multiple devices to find a single document or photo. You'll save time, and simultaneously reduce stress. Moreover, centralization provides peace of mind; knowing your important files exist in a cohesive structure reduces the risk of accidental loss or duplication. And, should you need to share or collaborate, you're already ahead with everything in place.

Laying the Foundation: Preparing for Centralization

Before consolidating, evaluate your current digital landscape. Start by listing where your files currently reside: explore your phone, laptop, external drives, and cloud services. Make a note of any accounts or services you use, such as Google Drive, Dropbox, iCloud, or OneDrive. This overview is your starting map. With understanding comes clarity; the list will highlight just how disparate your files are, and therein lies the motivation to move forward.

Now, consider your filing habits. Ask yourself: Do I often misplace files? Are some folders overflowing while others remain empty? Recognizing your patterns will help you shape a system that minimizes missteps and suits your preferences.

Crafting the Central Structure

Having a central system means all files are stored under one 'roof.' This doesn't mean one physical location, but a logical system of access and storage. Depending on your needs, you might choose a single cloud service or a hybrid between a primary cloud storage with local backups for sensitive files.

• Choose Your Primary Storage Location:

• For most, a reliable cloud service fits the bill. They offer accessible storage with ample space and sharing capabilities. Consider factors like potential data recovery, ease of access across devices, and security features.

• Establish a Consistent Folder Hierarchy:

• Design an intuitive folder system that reflects how you naturally categorize your files. For example, you may create top-level folders such as 'Personal,' 'Work,' 'Finances,' and 'Photos.' Each top-level folder can house subfolders (e.g., 'Photos' might include 'Vacations,' 'Events,' 'Family').

• Naming Conventions:

• Simplify searches by adopting consistent naming conventions. For example, for photos or documents: [Year]-[Month]-[Day]_Description (e.g., 2023-11-15_Family_Reunion).

• Regular Review and Maintenance:

• Set reminders for periodic checks—perhaps monthly or quarterly—to sift through your files and ensure they remain well-organized. Regularly delete duplicates and unnecessary files to free up space and maintain clarity.

Avoiding Common Mistakes

Awareness of common missteps can help prevent them. A frequent error is over-categorization, where too many folders make the system cumbersome. Remember, simplicity triumphs. Another pitfall is inconsistent use—starting well but reverting back to old habits out of convenience. Commitment to the system ensures long-term gains.

Practical Example: Consolidating Work Documents

Imagine you frequently find yourself hunting for important work documents scattered between your laptop, an old hard drive, and your company's shared Dropbox. Here's how you could consolidate:

• Select your centralized location. Choose a dedicated work folder within a reliable cloud service, such as Google Drive, keeping in mind company privacy and security protocols.

• Organize by project or client within that folder. Create subfolders for each project or client, and within those, further sub-divisions for 'Contracts,' 'Presentations,' 'Meeting Notes,' etc.

• Migrate existing documents. Set time aside to move your current documents to their new home. Ensure everything adheres to your new naming convention as you transition.

• Develop a habit of adding new documents directly. Cultivate the practice of saving documents directly to the correct location through prompts or shortcuts.

A Reflective Check-In

To keep your finger on the pulse of efficiency, occasionally ask yourself these questions:

• Have I noticed a reduction in time spent searching for files?

• Am I using the system consistently?

- Do I feel less stressed about my digital clutter?
- How could I improve the system further to fit any changing needs?

Final Thoughts: Embrace Digital Rightsizing

In establishing your centralized filing system, remember that the goal isn't just to reduce clutter, but to foster a heightened sense of digital well-being. With everything in its place, you'll enhance productivity, simplify file sharing, and invest time where it matters most—creating and enjoying rather than searching and sorting. As you embark on organizing your digital life, anticipate the fulfillment of clarity and order, knowing that each file has found its rightful home.

Chapter 11: Saving Time with Automation: How to Use Scripts and Shortcuts

The daily struggle with digital clutter is real. Files scattered everywhere on your desktop, misnamed documents, and those overwhelming digital folders of photos and projects—these all contribute to wasted hours. But what if those precious hours could be reclaimed by not doing certain tasks at all? Welcome to the world of automation, where scripts and shortcuts can transform your digital life into a model of efficiency and organization.

Understanding Automation: The Basics

Automation in the context of digital file organization refers to using tools and scripts to perform repetitive tasks without manual intervention. With the right setup, you can sort, rename, and move files with just a click, or even automatically. Imagine your downloads folder auto-clearing outdated files, or photos neatly archived into folders by date. Sounds like magic? It's closer to a very practical reality.

What You'll Need to Get Started:

- Understanding Your Workflow : Before diving in, get a handle on your file organization needs. Identify the most time-consuming tasks and reflect on what you do most frequently.
- Basic Tech Tools : Depending on your operating system, there are various built-in tools. On Windows, you might use PowerShell scripts, while Mac users can explore Automator or AppleScript. Additionally, cross-platform tools like Zapier or IFTTT can connect apps and automate online workflows.
- A Little Patience : Automation can require some setup time. Investing time initially will save you hours later.

Setting Up Your First Automation

Let's walk through setting up a basic automation on both Windows and Mac systems, tailored to auto-organize your Downloads folder.

For Windows Users: PowerShell Script

PowerShell offers robust scripting capabilities. Here's a simple guide for automating file organization:

- Identify File Types : Decide which files need organizing; for example, PDFs, images, and executables.
- Create Destination Folders : Organize your Downloads folder by type, e.g., \Downloads\PDFs\, \Downloads\Images\.
- Write a Simple Script :

Open PowerShell ISE and paste the following script template:

```powershell
$source = "C:\Users\YourUsername\Downloads"
$destinationPDF = "C:\Users\YourUsername\Downloads\PDFs\"
$destinationImages = "C:\Users\YourUsername\Downloads\Images\"
Move-Item -Path "$source\*.pdf" -Destination $destinationPDF
Move-Item -Path "$source\*.jpg" -Destination $destinationImages
Move-Item -Path "$source\*.png" -Destination $destinationImages
```

- Run Your Script : Execute it by selecting “Run” or using F5. Observe as your files jump into their new homes.
- Schedule Automation : Use Task Scheduler to run this script at regular intervals.

For Mac Users: Automator Workflow

Automator is your friend when it comes to crafting tailored file-management solutions:

- Start a New Workflow : Open Automator, choose “New Document,” and select “Folder Action”.
- Select the Downloads Folder : Link this action to your Downloads folder.
- Create the Action Steps :
- Filter Finder Items : Add a “Filter Finder Items” action, setting it to “Kind is Document”.
- Move Finder Items : Follow up with a “Move Finder Items” action to the desired folder, such as Documents.
- Test Your Workflow : Save and start downloading test files to see them whisked away into the right folders.
- Put It into Practice : Streamline new downloads with no further action.

Practical Application Examples

Beyond organizing your downloads, scripts and shortcuts can tackle numerous other digital chores:

- Batch Renaming Files : Use a script to rename batches of files with timestamps or project-specific keys. This reduces future headache when searching through archives.
- Sync and Backup : Set scripts to regularly back up documents to external drives or cloud storage like Google Drive, ensuring you never lose important files.
- Photo Management : An automation script can sort photos into folders by date or event, instantly readying them for sharing or archiving.

Avoiding Common Pitfalls

Automation is powerful, but like any good tool, it's crucial to wield it effectively:

- Over-Automating : Avoid the urge to automate everything. Prioritize repetitive tasks and ensure the automation enhances rather than complicates your workflow.
- Backup First : Especially when new to scripting, always have a complete backup. A misplaced script can accidentally move or delete files, so a safety net is imperative.
- Documentation : Keep a log of your scripts and automations. Should you need to revisit or adjust them, understanding what you did initially will save time and frustration.

A Reflection to Take Action

Now consider: What repetitive digital tasks eat into your day? List out these tasks and think about how they might be automated. Ask yourself how much time you could regain with just a small investment in setting these processes up.

Automation represents a leap into a more organized and less cluttered future. By incorporating scripts and shortcuts into your workflow, you manage your digital environment rather than merely coping with it. Remember, the key is to start small—implement one automation at a time and expand as you grow more confident. In little time, you'll be surprised at the load lifted from your digital life.

So, what will you automate next?

Chapter 12: Building a Routine: Daily Practices for Maintaining Digital Order

In a world where digital files accumulate at an unprecedented rate, maintaining order requires vigilance and regular care. Building a daily routine for digital organization is akin to tidying up your desk at the end of each workday—a simple yet impactful practice that prevents chaos from creeping back into your life. This chapter guides you through the essential daily practices to sustain your digital harmony.

Begin with a Daily Digital Check-In

Think of your daily digital check-in as taking inventory. Whether you start your day with it or wind down before bed, setting aside a small slice of time—ideally 10 to 15 minutes—can prevent digital clutter from piling up.

- Email Management : As emails flood your inbox, adopt a decisive approach:
- Immediately delete or archive messages that don't require action or retention.
- Respond to quick emails on the spot, flagging those needing more thoughtful replies.
- Direct essential emails to specific folders labeled by project or urgency.
- File Review and Sorting : At the end of your day, review downloads, screenshots, or any documents created:
- Move files to appropriate folders within your defined structure.
- Rename any files with clear, descriptive labels to make future retrieval a breeze.

These simple steps ensure you keep a handle on what might otherwise become an overwhelmingly unorganized jumble.

Enable Automation Wisely

Embracing technology that works for you is key to maintaining order without losing time. With a plethora of tools, aim for those that genuinely simplify your routines:

- Automated Backups : Set up daily backups of crucial folders to cloud services like Dropbox or Google Drive. Configure these to occur during downtime, so they don't disrupt your daily computer use.
- Email Filters and Rules : Establish filters to automatically sort incoming emails. For instance, redirect newsletters to a 'To Read Later' folder, allowing you to focus on mission-critical communications first.

Harnessing these tools helps your digital housekeeping run on autopilot, leaving you free to focus on tasks that require active attention.

The Digital Declutter Quick Sweep

Akin to a quick sweep of your physical workspace, a brief yet thorough scour through your digital devices can stave off future clutter headaches. Here's how you can delve in effectively each day:

- Desktop De-cluttering : Look at your computer desktop. If files or shortcuts scatter the screen, take a few moments to remove or file them appropriately.
- Smartphone Spring Clean : Skim through your phone at the day's end. Clear out temporary files, browse history, and cache from apps. Unsubscribe from unwanted notifications that clutter your screen and your focus.

This routine mini-decluttering ensures digital spaces remain pristine and functional, just like cleaning off a kitchen counter at day's end.

Reflect and Adjust

Maintaining digital order isn't a one-size-fits-all process. Reflect daily on what works and where friction occurs in your routine. Each day's bookmark should be a moment of reflection, giving you insight into refining your practices as you learn more about what you need and value.

- Reflective Queries : Ask yourself questions like:
- What took longer than expected to locate today?
- Did any files feel cumbersome to sort? Why?
- Have I used all the apps or tools I thought were essential?
- Adapt and Evolve : Use these reflections to fine-tune your system. If an app's automation isn't saving time, pivot to another. If a folder structure seems inconvenient, tweak it for clarity and efficiency.

Such introspection invigorates your routine, keeping it personalized and pragmatic, as unique as the digital life it supports.

Mini Exercise: Craft Your Routine

Take a few minutes now to sketch out what your digital organization routine might ideally look like. Jot down the tools you intend to use, the time you'll allocate daily, and the general order of activities. Perhaps it involves checking emails straight out of bed, or maybe it's a five-minute desktop declutter while waiting for your morning brew to steep. Keep this outline flexible; adjust over the coming weeks as your workflow and life require.

Common Pitfalls and How to Avoid Them

Even with the best intentions, roadblocks can appear. Recognize common mistakes and enhance your routine by knowing how to dodge them.

- Over-Organizing : Avoid creating excessively granular folder schemas that confuse rather than clarify. Stick to a simple, hierarchical structure tailored to your immediate needs.

• Forgetting the Routine : It's easy to brush off these routines when projects heat up or schedules tight. To combat this, set a daily reminder viewable when you check your calendar or emails.

• Ignoring File Naming : As projects evolve, messy and generic filenames become a tangle of confusion. Cultivate a habit of naming files clearly upon creation, and rename existing ones that lack clear identifiers.

Knowing these pitfalls arms you against them, helping streamline your efforts to maintain your digital space as a reservoir of order and efficiency.

By implementing these streamlined, daily practices and customizing them to suit your lifestyle, you instill digital discipline not as an obligation but as a natural part of your daily rhythm. Remember, maintaining digital order is not about perfection but consistency. With each day's effort, the cumulative effect is a more organized, stress-free digital existence that supports your goals—rather than hinder them.

Chapter 13: Advanced Techniques for Power Users: Version Control and Archiving

In the buzzing world of digital management, power users stand as the trailblazers, often needing robust, flexible, and advanced strategies to keep their workflows efficient. This chapter guides you through the sophisticated practices of version control and archiving—essential elements for anyone serious about digital file organization. With these tools, you can ensure your files are not just organized, but resilient and traceable as they evolve over time.

Understanding Version Control

Version control is the backbone of managing updates and changes to documents. Imagine it as a digital ledger that records every alteration, allowing you to retrieve past versions if needed. This is particularly useful when collaborating on projects or when refining creative work.

Practical Example : Imagine you're a freelance graphic designer. A client requests a series of changes to a brochure design. Without version control, you'd likely overwrite the original file or save versions haphazardly, causing confusion about which file is the most recent or retains specific elements.

Here, version control software like Git or cloud services such as Google Drive and OneDrive can be invaluable, tracking changes in real-time. For personal document management, they may seem excessive, but understanding their potential can expand your digital toolkit.

Setting Up a Personal Version Control System

While professional version control systems cater primarily to software developers, these principles can be adapted for personal use:

- Choose Your Tool : If your work involves heavy text or code edits, consider Git. For document and media file management, utilize features in Dropbox, Google Drive, or OneDrive, which auto-save revisions without manual input.
- Develop a Naming Convention : Consistent naming aids clarity. A simple format like project_name_v1, project_name_v2 can help track progression at a glance.
- Regular Commits/Saves : Instead of overwriting files, save new versions with updates. In a cloud-based environment, enable auto-sync to capture every change.

Archive Like a Pro

Archiving differs from mere backup by re-organizing inactive files into a systematic storage. When files no longer need immediate access but might be required for reference or compliance, they become candidates for archiving.

Reflective Prompt : Consider your email inbox. How often do you search back a year or more to find an old message? This type of retrieval, when extended to all file types, underscores the utility of a well-organized archive.

Steps to Effective Archiving

- Evaluate and Cull : Not all files warrant archiving. Determine what to archive based on criteria like legal necessity, historical importance, or personal value.
- Choose Suitable Digital Formats : Convert files into formats that are widely used and backward compatible, such as PDF for documents or MP3 for audio, ensuring access remains intact over time.
- Decide Storage Solution :
- External Hard Drives : Good for large data but ensure they are stored in a safe environment.
- Cloud Storage : Services like Backblaze or AWS Glacier offer low-cost options that ensure files remain accessible and secure.
- Establish a Schedule : Regular archiving schedules prevent file clutter and ensure recent yet non-essential items are archived promptly.

Common Mistakes to Avoid

- Over-Archiving : Not every revised draft needs archiving. Be ruthless in discerning what truly matters in the long term.
- Neglecting Metadata : Proper metadata tagging at the time of archiving makes future retrieves easier. Consider tagging by year, project name, or category.
- Ignoring File Redundancy : Unchecked duplicates can clog archives. Use de-duplication tools before archiving to maintain cleanliness.

Checklist for Ongoing Management

- [ ] Setup and adhere to a clear version control naming system.
- [ ] Identify which files are critical for archiving.
- [ ] Schedule a quarterly review of files to determine archival candidates.
- [ ] Regularly audit archived data to ensure relevance and remove obsolete files.
- [ ] Back up archives separately to mitigate data loss from accidental deletion.

Reader Example: Streamlining Creative Workflows

Consider Susie, a fiction writer who frequently revisits and revises her manuscripts. By implementing version control, she feels empowered to experiment without the fear of losing her best ideas. Through persistent archiving, she maintains a digital library of her writings, safeguarding them for future compilation—an endeavor made smoother by her methodical organization.

For power users like you, understanding and utilizing advanced file organization techniques can open doors to greater productivity and peace of mind. Embrace these concepts, and weave them into your routine. The clarity and competence they bring to your digital experience are invaluable, ensuring your files evolve seamlessly and remain at your beck and call.

Chapter 14: Sharing and Collaborating: Efficiently Managing Shared Files and Folders

In today's digital workspace, sharing documents and photos has become second nature. While it offers remarkable convenience and fosters collaboration, managing shared files efficiently remains a daunting task for many. Whether it's family albums shared in a cloud drive, or business documents in collaborative workspaces, mastering the art of sharing can drastically improve both personal organization and professional productivity.

Understanding the Basics

Before diving into strategies, it's essential to understand the platforms commonly used for sharing files. These include Google Drive, Dropbox, Microsoft OneDrive, and dedicated project management tools like Slack or Trello. Each platform has its own set of sharing features, permissions, and collaboration tools.

Google Drive is known for its seamless integration with other Google services. You can share a single document or an entire folder, adjusting permissions for viewing, commenting, or editing.

Dropbox offers straightforward sharing with links that can be set to view-only or allow for edits. It's particularly useful for sharing large files that exceed email attachment limits.

Microsoft OneDrive integrates well with Office apps, making it an ideal choice for those heavily reliant on Word, Excel, and PowerPoint. It allows for specific access permissions to be set for uploaded files.

The common thread among these platforms is the ability to tailor access: decide who views the files, who can edit them, and who receives notifications for changes.

Setting Up Your Shared Spaces

Creating a shared organizational structure is critical. Start by identifying your key collaborative projects. For instance, if you're managing a family photo archive, set up a dedicated folder labeled "Family Photos." Within this, subfolders for each year or event can keep the collection orderly.

For work documents, create a main folder for each project. Within each project, have subfolders for "Drafts," "Finals," and "Resources." Maintaining separate folders for various stages of documents aids in easily locating the necessary files and reduces clutter.

Permissions: A Double-Edged Sword

One common pitfall in file sharing is overlooking permissions and access rights. Sharing a document without proper consideration can lead to unauthorized edits or accidental data losses. Always adjust sharing settings to align with your intended level of collaboration.

Here's a simple checklist:

- Viewer : For those who need to read the document but not make changes.
- Commenter : Ideal for collaborative environments where feedback is necessary but control over the main content needs to remain with specific individuals.
- Editor : Best for teams working actively on files, ensuring everyone can make necessary changes.

Handling permissions with care prevents chaos in documents and ensures everyone remains aligned with the project goals. Regular audits of who has access to what can help avoid future issues.

Communicating Changes

When files are shared among various contributors, communication becomes key. Implementing a clear protocol on how updates and changes are communicated prevents overlapping work and ensures all team members are on the same page.

Tips for Smooth Communication:

- Use platform-specific alerts to notify team members of updates.
- Establish conventions for file naming, such as appending the date or version number to the file name.
- Encourage the use of comments for minor suggestions rather than directly altering documents. Tools like Google Docs 'suggesting mode' are invaluable here.

Managing Versions

Version control is an often-overlooked aspect of file sharing that can save teams from rework. Platforms like Google Drive and OneDrive have built-in version history features that allow you to access previous versions of a document, which can be a lifesaver when errors occur.

Practical Strategies:

- Regularly label file versions and utilize version history to track changes over time.
- Avoid making extensive changes without version tagging; this precaution can save you from reverting to old versions after significant edits.
- When in doubt, duplicate the document before making major changes to maintain an easy-to-access backup.

Preventing Common Pitfalls

A few common missteps can derail your file sharing and collaboration efforts. Avoid the following:

- Overlooking permissions : Regularly review who has access to your files. As teams change, so should file permissions.
- Ignoring platform updates : Tools frequently update their systems, introducing new features that might improve your workflow. Stay informed to leverage these improvements.
- Lack of backup : Even cloud files can be accidentally deleted. Keep backups for crucial documents.

Reflecting and Adjusting

No organizational strategy is perfect from the get-go. After implementing a sharing strategy, reflect periodically on its effectiveness. Gather feedback from collaborators and make adjustments as necessary. Consider questions like:

- How often do files get misplaced?
- Are team members able to access what they need without hassle?
- Is the version control process working smoothly?

By regularly assessing the system, you keep it alive and responsive to changes in team dynamics or project needs.

A Warm Reminder

As you cultivate your skills in managing shared digital spaces, remember the balance between openness and control. Sharing files is not just about accessibility; it's about creating an environment where collaboration can thrive securely and efficiently. By setting up well-organized systems, maintaining mindful oversight over permissions, and fostering clear communication, you'll foster a collaborative atmosphere that supports creativity and productivity for all involved.

Chapter 15: Digital Security and Privacy: Protecting Your Data After Organizing

Congratulations on getting your digital files sorted! Whether you've tucked those documents into neatly labeled folders or finally made sense of your burgeoning photo collection, you've taken a significant step forward in digital file organization. However, organization is only part of the battle. To truly protect your digital life, it's essential to prioritize the security and privacy of your data. Let's delve into some practical strategies that can help keep your information safe from cyber threats.

Understand the Risks

First, let's discuss why security and privacy are so critical. With files neatly organized, they are accessible not just by you but potentially by others if your systems aren't secure. Here are a few scenarios you want to avoid:

- Unauthorized access by hackers who can exploit your personal data for identity theft.
- Malware infections that can corrupt files or lock you out of your own data until you pay a ransom.
- Accidental breaches where sensitive information may become publicly accessible due to poor sharing settings.

Basic Security Measures

The foundation of digital security lies in implementing basic protective measures:

- Use Strong Passwords: A strong password is your first line of defense. Use a mix of uppercase, lowercase, numbers, and special characters. Tools like LastPass or Dashlane can help manage and generate strong passwords.
- Enable Two-Factor Authentication (2FA): This adds a layer of security by requiring a second form of identification, such as a text message or an authentication app.
- Install Reliable Antivirus Software: Ensure that your antivirus program is updated regularly to protect against the latest threats.

Cloud Storage: A Double-Edged Sword

Many people organize digital files using cloud services like Google Drive, Dropbox, or iCloud. While immensely convenient, they present unique security challenges. Here's how to secure your cloud storage:

- Review and Adjust Privacy Settings: Go through each setting on your cloud platform. Disable sharing for folders that contain sensitive information.
- Audit Shared Files Regularly: Keep track of what you've shared and with

whom. Revoke access if it's no longer needed.

• Use Encryption for Sensitive Files: Services like Boxcryptor and Cryptomator allow for end-to-end encryption, ensuring that even if the storage service is compromised, your data remains private.

Secure Your Devices

Your digital files can also be vulnerable due to unsecured devices:

• Keep Your Software Updated: Regular updates patch security vulnerabilities, so enable automatic updates for your operating system and all applications.

• Use Screensaver Passwords: It might seem minor, but requiring a password after inactivity helps prevent unauthorized physical access.

• Back-Up Your Data: Regular backups either on an external hard drive or another secured cloud service prevent data loss from hardware failures or ransomware attacks.

Common Missteps and How to Avoid Them

Even with the best intentions, certain practices can leave cracks in your security:

• Overconfidence in Built-in Security Features: Don't assume that default settings on applications or cloud services are adequate. Always customize settings to fit your security needs.

• Sharing With Too Many Permissions: When sharing files or folders, use 'view only' access unless it's absolutely necessary for others to have editing privileges.

Mini Process: Conduct a Security Audit

Here's a simple process to give your digital security a checkup:

• List Devices and Accounts: Write down every device, app, or service you use regularly.

• Review Last Update: Check when each device or app was last updated.

• Analyze Sharing Permissions: Look at which files are shared and adjust settings where necessary.

• Check for Unused Accounts/Logins: Close accounts you no longer use. Keeping dormant accounts increases your exposure risk.

Exercise: Create a Security Strategy

Developing your own security strategy doesn't have to be complex. Start with setting personal security goals. Perhaps it's re-evaluating your password strategy or learning to use encryption software more effectively. Write down realistic actions and check them off as you progress.

Quick Checklist to Enhance Security

• [ ] Update all passwords to strong, unique combinations.

• [ ] Enable two-factor authentication where possible.

• [ ] Conduct a privacy settings audit of cloud storage accounts.

• [ ] Install reliable antivirus and ensure automatic updates are turned on.

• [ ] Regularly back up vital files to different locations.

Reflection Prompt

Think about your most sensitive files. What would be the consequences if they were accessed by unauthorized persons? Having this awareness can drive the discipline needed to maintain a high level of security.

In wrapping up this chapter, remember that while organizing your digital life begins with sorting and labeling, securing that life demands ongoing diligence. The digital world offers us incredible convenience but not without risk. Each step you take towards securing your digital files is a step towards safeguarding your privacy and ensuring peace of mind. Stay vigilant, stay informed, and keep your digital environment as secure as your physical one.

Chapter 16: Troubleshooting: What to Do When Organization Systems Break Down

Even the best-laid plans can falter. As you set up and maintain your digital file organization system, you're bound to encounter hiccups, confusion, or moments of complete chaos. Recognizing and recovering from these breakdowns can transform a minor setback into an opportunity to refine your method. Here, we'll address common pitfalls and provide practical strategies to help you get back on track.

Symptoms of a Broken System

Sometimes, the signs of a disrupted system are glaringly obvious—a disorganized folder structure, files saved in random locations, or overwhelming cloud storage full of duplicates. Start by identifying these common symptoms:

- Files scattered across multiple locations: Instead of having a designated folder or drive for specific files, they are spread out, making it hard to find what you need.
- Inconsistent naming conventions: When folder and file names don't follow your chosen system, it becomes challenging to search and retrieve them.
- Outdated or unused files cluttering space: Old files often accumulate and consume valuable storage space, making it hard to discern what's essential.
- Uncontrolled versioning issues: Multiple copies of the same document lead to confusion and potential errors.

Recognition is the first step. Now, let's focus on fixing these issues.

Recovering Clarity with a Sorting Session

Once you identify that your system has veered off course, take immediate action with a structured sorting session. Here's a mini process to streamline this task:

- Schedule uninterrupted time: Set aside a specific window, even if it's just an hour, to solely focus on tidying up your digital space.
- Prioritize problematic areas: Choose one unruly section at a time, such as misplaced documents or mismanaged photos, and tackle it first.
- Create temporary folders: As you sift through files, temporarily place them in broad categories like "To Sort," "Old Versions," or "Duplicates." This helps in systematically addressing each subsection without overwhelming yourself.
- Rename and relocate: As you handle each file, ensure it has a standardized name. Then, move it to its appropriate folder following the original organizational framework you chose.

Dealing with Inconsistent Naming Conventions

Naming consistency is crucial for both searchability and sanity. Review the inconsistent naming patterns and decide on an improved approach. Here are some practical tips:

- Set a Standard Naming Format: Define a format and stick to it. For instance, use "YYYY-MM-DD_Event_Description" for document and photo naming.
- Implement Batch Renaming Tools: For existing files, consider using batch renaming software. These tools can help you update file names en masse based on your chosen conventions.
- Create a Naming Cheat Sheet: Outline your naming conventions in a simple document. This cheatsheet can guide you and others who access the system in maintaining consistency.

Streamlining with Regular Maintenance

Preventative maintenance can significantly reduce the likelihood of system breakdowns over time. Adopt regular upkeep habits to keep digital clutter at bay:

- Weekly Review Sessions: Dedicate a short session each week to quickly review and sort recent downloads, emails, and other documents, moving them to their proper places.
- Monthly Deep Dives: Go beyond the surface once a month by thoroughly checking various sections of your system for misplaced or duplicate files.
- Utilize Automation Tools: Leverage automated features like rule-based file sorting or document cloud syncing. These can drastically cut down on manual sorting time.

Exercise: Audit Your Digital System

Having a regular routine is great, but sometimes it's essential to perform a deeper audit. Try this exercise to get a clearer picture of where your system stands:

- List Three Problematic Areas: Write down the sections of your digital life that bring the most stress or confusion.
- Evaluate Access Patterns: For each area, consider how often you need to access these files and how difficult it usually is.
- Identify One Immediate Fix: Identify one actionable step for each problem area. This might be consolidating folders, emptying a cluttered downloads folder, or simply archiving seldom-used documents.
- Reflect on System Longevity: Ask yourself if your current system meets your needs for both present use and future growth. Identify areas that may need structural changes.

Final Thoughts: Embrace Adaptability

Remember, a perfectly functioning digital organization system doesn't exist. It evolves as your needs and technology change. Allow yourself the flexibility to tweak your system and explore new tools and methods that may enhance efficiency. Encourage everyone involved to provide feedback on what's working and what's not, and consider it carefully.

Developing a practical, adaptable approach to system failures will not only help you address current issues but will also arm you with strategies to face future challenges. Your goal is not perfection but rather continuous improvement. With diligence and a proactive mindset, you'll navigate any breakdown with confidence, ensuring that your digital world remains an asset, not a burden.

Chapter 17: Developing a Personal Maintenance Plan: Keeping Your Digital World in Check

In today's fast-paced digital landscape, maintaining an organized and efficient digital environment isn't just beneficial; it's essential. Systems are only as good as your ability to sustain them, and like a well-tended garden, your digital files need regular attention to flourish. Let's dive into creating a personal maintenance plan that will not only keep your digital world ticking like clockwork but also free you from the constant clutter headache.

Understanding Your Digital Ecosystem

Before setting up a maintenance routine, it's crucial to understand your digital ecosystem. Consider the variety of files you handle daily: photos, documents, emails, applications, and cloud storage. Each of these has its own way of creeping into disarray. Reflect on your current habits:

- Which types of files cause you the most stress?
- Where do you regularly lose track of important documents?
- How often do you truly need to access certain files, and which can be archived or deleted?

Jot down these points, noting the particular areas where you feel overwhelmed. This will guide your focus areas for maintenance.

Set Realistic Maintenance Intervals

The cornerstone of any maintenance plan is setting realistic intervals for action. A common mistake is to over-schedule tasks, leading to maintenance fatigue. Here's a simple framework you can adapt:

- Daily Tasks : Spend 5-10 minutes tidying your desktop and closing unnecessary tabs or applications. Delete or file emails that won't need further response.
- Weekly Tasks : Allocate 30 minutes to review pending downloads, organize new documents into their respective folders, and empty recycle bins or trash.
- Monthly Tasks : Dedicate an hour to backing up essential files to an external drive or cloud service, and perform software updates to keep your systems secure and efficient.
- Quarterly Tasks : Plan a more extensive review session for about 90 minutes. This is when you can clear out unused applications, reorganize photo collections, and assess storage usage across different platforms.

Mini Exercise: Weekly Ritual

To ease into this maintenance habit, start with a simple weekly ritual. Set aside a regular time each week, perhaps Saturday morning with a cup of coffee. Decide that this is your maintenance time, a moment to bond with your digital space instead of dreading it. During this session, follow these mini-steps:

- Quickly scan recent files for duplicates and delete them.
- Rename any documents that have nonsensical or default titles.
- Move any items from your desktop to their appropriate long-term folder.

Consistency is the key here. Once entrenched in your routine, it becomes less of a chore and more a natural extension of your weekly rhythm.

Common Pitfalls and How to Avoid Them

Even with the best of intentions, it's easy to get sidetracked. Here's how you can navigate some common pitfalls without losing steam:

- Over-Complication : Avoid creating overly complex filing systems. Your files should be no more than three clicks away. If a folder doesn't have at least ten files, it likely needs reconsideration or merging.
- Procrastination : Major reorganizations can often lead to delay. Break tasks into smaller chunks and aim for progress over perfection. If the task seems daunting, remind yourself there's no deadline; consistency beats rapidity.
- Neglecting Old Systems : As new technology and systems become part of your routine, it's easy to forget older data storage methods. Make it part of your quarterly routine to migrate or archive data from old systems to prevent obsolescence.

Checklist for a Healthy Digital Environment

- Establish and write down a schedule for your maintenance intervals.
- Utilize technology as an ally: calendar reminders, automated backup services, and organizational apps can reduce the manual load.
- Set aside time for occasional digital clean-up marathons, where you delve into archives and ensure they're still relevant.
- Regularly update security measures and applications to protect your data integrity.

Reflect and Adjust

Remember, there is no one-size-fits-all or 'perfection' in digital organization. Your lifestyle, work needs, and technology use will evolve. Return periodically to the points you noted at the beginning, reassessing what works and what doesn't.

- What aspects of your system bring relief or added strain?
- Have your digital needs shifted, requiring an adjustment in your plan?

Schedule a bi-annual reflection. A quick review every six months allows you to tweak your system based on evolving needs. A maintenance plan should serve you, not the other way around.

Embrace Continuous Learning

The digital world is in constant flux, with new tools and methods emerging regularly. Keep an eye out for innovations or features that can assist your file management efficiency. Joining online communities or forums can offer fresh perspectives and tips from fellow digital organizers, enhancing your personal plan.

By developing a personal maintenance plan, you're investing in peace of mind and productivity. With a bit of forethought and regular attention, your digital ecosystem can remain as robust and orderly as any physical filing system, ensuring that technology serves as an asset rather than an obstacle. As you stroll through your digital garden, enjoy the neat rows and thriving folders that make your digital life as calming as a well-kept paradise.

Chapter 18: Future-Proofing Your System: Adapting to Technological Changes and Growth

In the ever-evolving landscape of technology, staying ahead of the curve might seem like a daunting task, especially when it comes to organizing your digital files. However, future-proofing your organizational system is not just about chasing the latest app or hardware; it's about creating a flexible framework that can evolve with new technologies. If you're wondering how to ensure your digital filing system remains robust and efficient, you're in the right place.

Embrace Flexibility in Your System

The cornerstone of future-proofing is flexibility. When initially setting up a digital organization system, it's easy to cling to tools and methods that feel comfortable. Yet, predictability can lead to stagnation.

Instead, consider these flexible practices:

- File Naming Conventions: Develop a naming convention that can evolve. Prefix your files with the year and project (e.g., 2023_ProjectName_Description) to adapt easily if your priorities change in the future.
- Folder Hierarchies: Keep your folder structures shallow. Deep hierarchies make it challenging to locate files when migration to a new system. Focus on broad categories that are intuitive and can accommodate new types of files and formats.

Regularly Schedule Review Sessions

As mundane as it sounds, scheduling regular reviews of your digital filing system can be transformative. Technology changes rapidly, and a system that worked two years ago might be less effective today.

During your review:

- Evaluate Cloud Storage Providers: Is your current provider still your best option? Assess factors like storage needs, security features, and integrational capacity with other tools you use.
- Audit Software and Tools: Organize an inventory of the tools you've employed. Check if any have fallen into disuse or if there are better, more integrated options available.

Invest in Knowledge and Skill Development

Being proactive involves continuously educating yourself about emerging technologies. While this doesn't mean becoming an expert coder, understanding the basics can significantly enhance your capability to adapt.

• Enroll in Online Courses or Workshops: Platforms like Coursera or LinkedIn Learning often offer short courses focused on digital productivity tools and technological trends.

• Join Online Tech Communities: Engage in forums or groups related to digital organization. Discussions often highlight emerging trends and tools that you might find useful.

Opt for Interoperable Tech

A central tenet of future-proofing is choosing technology that plays well with others. Interoperable tech ensures that your ecosystems — apps, devices, and cloud storage — can communicate with each other seamlessly.

Look for:

• APIs and Integration Capabilities: Ensure your tools can connect with other leading apps. For instance, note-taking apps that sync with your cloud storage can save time.

• Cross-Platform Compatibility: Devices and applications should work across your operating systems. This means an app or software can be used on both an Android phone and a Windows laptop without losing functionality.

Scalable Storage Solutions

As your digital life expands, so too will your need for storage. Opt for cloud services that offer scalable storage solutions. This does not just mean being able to store more but also doing so efficiently.

• Tiered Storage Plans: Choose providers that offer variety in their storage plans. This flexibility can save you money as you pay for exactly what you need and easily upgrade when necessary.

• Efficient Data Management Tools: Tools like deduplication software can help manage storage use effectively by eliminating duplicate files without risking data loss.

Practical Steps to Minimize Risk

Adapting to new technology carries inherent risks. However, you can minimize these risks with precautious steps:

• Regular Backups: Create a schedule for backing up your critical data. Ensure that backups are stored in both local (e.g., external hard drives) and cloud storages.

• Version Control: Use version control systems to manage changes effectively, particularly for documents that are frequently updated.

• Protect Against Obsolescence: If you rely on specific tech or file formats ensure they won't become obsolete. Convert fragile files to more widely accepted formats when necessary or invest in viewer tools for legacy documents.

Reflection Prompts for Long-Term Success

Here are some questions to help you assess and refine your digital organization strategy:

- How easily can I adapt my file organization to a new system or tool?
- Am I maximizing my current technological investments, or are there areas I haven't fully explored?
- What are the emerging trends in digital organization that could benefit me in the short and long term?

Experimentation: Embrace Trial and Error

Finally, remember that future-proofing your digital organization is not a one-size-fits-all endeavor. Every individual's needs are different, which is why experimenting is crucial.

- Trial New Tools: Dedicate time to experimenting with new applications or systems. Start small by trialing them in non-critical areas, and evaluate their performance before integrating them more broadly.
- Keep What Works Like Charm: While trying out the latest technologies, keep the components of your system that prove agelessly efficient.

By embracing these strategies, you can develop a digital organization system that not only meets your current needs but adapts seamlessly as those needs—and technologies—evolve. While technology is a moving target, your readiness to anticipate and adjust to these changes can make all the difference in creating a future-ready digital life.

About the Author

T. S. AVINI is a writer who believes in the power of sharing life's lessons. Having faced hardship and pain, he turned to writing as a form of self-expression and healing. Today, he pours his heart into every book, aiming to help others navigate their own struggles and find strength in vulnerability.